Ebonie

Brytnie Devon Jones

BookLeaf Publishing

Presentation by *BookLeaf Publishing*

Web: www.bookleafpub.com

E-mail: info@bookleafpub.com

ISBN: 9789357442312

First edition 2023

I dedicate this book to all the 20-somethings and all the Black men and women who are living everyday doing the best that they can, to all the moms taking it day by day and to the hopeless romantics.

Blackity Black

From sew-ins and press outs to afros and box
braids
My blackness became my daily outfit
My source of pride.

R&B and Hip-Hop was the soundtrack
Black excellence excellently
Exuding my skin through the scent of
Shea butter and jojoba oil.

I only accept Black spelled with a capital B,
RESPEK my identity,
I am Black and Woman,
Woman and Black,
A Black Woman!

NOT SOLD SEPARATELY!

Black Queen

Dear Black Queen,
You act as if you don't know who you are…

Like Ntozake Shange didn't say,
"where there is a woman,
there is magic"

Like Maya didn't tell you that were a
"Phenomenal Woman"

Like grandma didn't teach you no home training

Didn't you listen when Jill Scott told you,
"You were a prized possession and
that everybody wasn't worthy"

Girl ain't mama ever told you that you were
special

Dear Black Queen,
You are a Queen,
I hope you'll remember that someday.

Freedom Ain't Free

Freedom.
A foreign concept.
I never once in my life felt free.
Not being Black.
Not being a woman.
Not as a 20-something.

I heard freedom ain’t free -
But I wonder if that shit even exist?

In-Between

Somewhere between loving myself and finding myself.

Competition

I wish I didn't feel like I was in competition with
women I've never met,
but only seen on the internet.

Wish I didn't constantly feel inferior to your old
friends
and ex-girlfriends back home
that you can't seem to dismiss.

Wish I didn't feel like if you had to choose
between me and them...
you'd choose them in a heartbeat
and up and leave me -
ALONE!

You'd be gone with not so much of a
"I'll always love you" or "You'll always be my
favorite girl".

I can't lie I'm feeling insecurities that I thought I
had buried away,
because I thought you pictured life with me,
but something's holding you back from me.

I wish I didn't feel like I was in competition with
women I've never met,
but have only seen on the internet.

I wish you loved me as much as I love you!

Fairytales & White Picket Fences

Someone once told me that I believed in
fairytales,
romance novels and white picket fences.

Someone once told me that I needed to grow up
AND stop thinking love is sunshine and roses.

Someone once told me that I was no longer the
same woman that made them fall in love.

They were right!

Maybe I'm naïve but I believe that love
can heal the deepest scars and the sharpest
wombs.

I believe that love is the type of magic
that can light your soul on fire.

I believe that love is the most powerful emotion.

I believe in love.

Fairytales and white picket fences are a bonus!

Message

There is a lot to say about a person who
encounters pain
after pain but can still find a reason to smile.

I Deserve Bettter

I’m too good for you
AND
I know I deserve better,
but I don’t want better,
because better isn’t you.

You know you’ll hurt me again,
and I know it too,
because I’m just too good for you..
And you know it too.

I will always love you no matter
how hard it is for me and you.
And I know you'll always love me too.

But I deserve better.
And I know better.
Better knows it too!

A Letter to Grandma

You loved men unconditionally who didn't
know how to love you.

Painted full canvases of yourself for ones who
only offered puzzle pieces
and allowed temporary lovers to overstay their
welcome.

You spoke life and prosperity into men who
ONLY spoke broken promises,
men who only caused you pain,
and knew how to love you black, blue and
speechless.

You mothered children by men who barely knew
how to take care of themselves.
How could they possibly take care of another
human or
a woman as delicate as you?

You loved men who temporarily erased your
childhood memories of pain and trauma and
made you feel like a woman;
made you lose all inhibitions.

You loved men who didn’t make it their mission
to wipe away your tears at night...
who didn’t aim to love you in the way you
deserved
and desired to be loved.

You loved men who unfortunately didn’t know
how to love you back.

You were served a bad deck of cards and never
received a lesson in
how real love is supposed to feel.

Somewhere along the way you lost you!
And I wish I could've been the one to save you!

Because you loved men who didn't deserve you!

God In You

There was once a moment in time when I held you on a pedestal.

Treated you like God -
even on days when there seemed to be no God in you!

You could do no wrong!

I told you that I'd never leave you,
that I trusted you,
that I'd ride for you,
hell that I'd die for you.

I accepted all of your flaws,
and told that I loved you.

I hoped you understood the risk that I was taking.

Guess I didn't understand the risk that I had taken.

The worst thing I could have done was find "home" in you,

because you didn't know what it took to make a house a home.

Good Girls

Mama said she wish that I was married first,
because that's what good Christian girls
are supposed to do.

First comes love, then comes marriage and then
comes babies.
That's the proper order.

But here I am covered in sin -
a baby and no ring.

Shame.

Mama said she wanted me to be better than her,
but I wanted to be just like her, because
she was the best mom I could ever ask for.

Black Boys in America

I wept for you,
because I knew there was a little
Black boy nestled in my stomach
waiting to enter the world.

I imagined your brown skin.

And I knew that you would be the
best thing to ever happen to me.

I knew that you would be perfect
in every way. BEYOND my wildest dreams.

But I still cried for you,
because I knew that you may
not get a fair shot in this world.

Even though I already love you endlessly,
I know America isn't too fond of you.

Black boys in America.

Even though they don't know you,
they will try to make a villain out of you.

I wept for you because I will make it my mission
to
fight for every little Black boy like you.

Every Black boy deserves to grow old,
deserves to be free in their skin...
deserves to live happily ever after.

I hope you know that mama will always
be here for you.

Cheering you on and rooting
for all the Black boys like you.

I hope you know that I'll raise hell
if anything was to ever happen to you.

I'll kick and scream and shout your name to
the rooftop until they remember you!

Black boys in America don't get to make it to
old, but I promise as your mama, I'm going to
die
before I witness my Black boy become a
headline
and known as just another Black boy in
America.

Remember Me

I hope you find the heart to love me on my
worse days
and to still love me when I leave your heart full
of disappointment.

I'm not always patient,
I'm not always smiling,
I'm not always laughing,
but I hope you remember my smiles more than
my frowns.

I hope you remember my laughs more than my
tears.

I hope you remember my love and the days we
played,
more than the days when I let frustration make
me yell.

I hope you remember that you were the best part
of my everyday and
your hugs and kisses made the air lighter and
easier to breathe.

I hope you remember that everything I ever did
was for you.
I hope you remember that I loved you more than
life itself.

Soundtrack

I’m the Nina to your Darius -
only reversed.
I’ll be your muse,
while you
capture me through your lens,
I’ll paint you a poetic picture.
I promise, I’m dope with this pen.

I’m the Syd to your Dre -
no roles switched.
You’re hip hop and I’m the perfect verse
over a tight beat.

I’m the Monica to your Quincy -
except I don’t want to have to end up playing
you for your heart,
I want to already own it.
I want to already know where you stand with
me.

I'm the soundtrack to your favorite 90's movie.
Unforgettable.

Say Their Names

They didn't have to shoot Breonna Taylor that day.

Another unarmed Black woman,
minding her business.

That Black woman lost her life and the streets were silent
for weeks until they weren't.

We stood in the middle of the streets with our street signs
demanding you to "SAY HER NAME",
because her name speaks volumes in these streets.

Her name will forever go down in history as an unarmed, young,
Black woman asleep in her bed.
A woman who took her last breathe in her sleep.

These white officers don't give a fuck about you and me.

Black man.

Black woman.

Black.

Black is all they see.

And when they see me and you -
they'd rather kill us in the street.

I wonder if she had a feeling that March 13
would be her last day on this earth?
I wonder if she too, wanted to call out for her
mama like George Floyd.

9 minutes. 29 seconds.

That's how long they knelt on your neck. That's
how long they disregarded your human life
and continued to commit murder in front of a
live audience.

9 minutes. 29 seconds.

All for a $20 bill. Who knew $20 was worth a
whole life?

Say Their Names.

Breonna Taylor.

George Floyd.

I'm sorry that you lost your lives as a result of being Black in America.

3 a.m.

You walked through the front door at 3 a.m.
And there I was...
waiting.

I needed to know that you were in one piece,
otherwise there would be no peace for me
tonight.

You walked through the front door at 3 a.m.
And I sighed in relief.

Then I rolled over and went to sleep.

No One Warned Me

No one warned me of the suffocation.

No one told me that my body wouldn't be my own.

No one told me that my thoughts would be discredited.

They didn't tell me that my success would have to be linked to man for it to be respected.

No one told me that my body would be a topic of discussion for every man in America.

No one told me that if I wore too little I was asking for "it" and if I wore too much I would be a "nun".

No one told me that if I was too serious, I would be called "mean",
or labeled the "angry Black woman" but if I was too nice, I would be called a push-over or naïve.

They didn't tell me that being a woman was a constant fight.

Why do I still feel like somebody's property?

A shell inside my own body.

No one warned me.

That Being a woman was equivalent to being a slave.

Bonus

Silence -
Locked up.

It's like I'm in a mental confinement,
I'm so stuck.

I want to say something but I can't,
seems as if you just lucked up!

Your words speak volumes and I ACTED
as if it didn't bother me but it did.

I guess I'm so used to pretending that I'm
confused on how to be real. I'm a porcelain doll
in a permanent package, perfectly sealed, mute!

I'm your punching bag...I let you say whatever
you want to say to me and I just sit there
SILENT!

I'm playing this game called LIFE.
It's either I win or I fail, I'm stuck in this shell.

I want to say something but I can't so I bottle it
all in

and when it's all over I press replay and
everything I could
or should have said I start to say.

I have trust issues so please excuse the tissues.
It's just that I let my emotions get the best of me,
and I emotionally exploded.

I'm stuck playing this game called LIFE,
without a strategy,
and no this is not another tragedy.

It's just a story about a girl who has no backbone
of her own.

So I stand in the mirror scared by my own
reflection,
because I don't like who I'm becoming.

I'm your personal test dummy, a toy for you to
toy with, a puppet!

You dressed up as one thing but you're really
another,
you're a MANNEQUIN!

I'm stuck playing this game called LIFE.

In the word LIFE, you have the word "if"
because life is "iffy",
and sometimes tricky.

Everything doesn't always work out that's why
at the end of boyfriend
and friend, you have the word "end",
because people are flaky and life is shaky.
And nothing is always like is seems.

Just when everything seems right, something
goes wrong.
It's like a bad love song.

But everything happens for a reason and in its
season.

My successes will outweigh my failures.

My past is a piece of the puzzle that leads to my
future,
and I'm striving to be the best and nothing or no
one can stop me,
because I'm confident and I'm determined.

I'm a leader, not a follower.

So follow me as I'm molded, sculpted and
shaped

into the WOMAN I'm supposed to be,
because I'm not your ordinary painted picture.

I'm an original, a masterpiece, a limited edition.

Follow me as I travel through stages and
different chapters,
but I know it won't be easy...
because I'm stuck playing this game called
LIFE!

www.ingramcontent.com/pod-product-compliance
Lightning Source LLC
Chambersburg PA
CBHW051754130826
49812CB00033B/1142
* 9 7 8 9 3 5 7 4 4 2 3 1 2 *